GREAT SCIENTISTS

WANGARI MAATHAI

WAYLAND

First published in Great Britain in 2025
by Wayland
Copyright © Hodder and Stoughton, 2025

All rights reserved
Editors: Amy Pimperton and Sarah Peutrill
Designer: Lisa Peacock

ISBN (HB): 978 1 5263 2855 7
ISBN (PB): 978 1 5263 2856 4

Printed and bound in Dubai

Wayland, an imprint of
Hachette Children's Group
Part of Hodder and Stoughton
Carmelite House
50 Victoria Embankment
London EC4Y 0DZ
An Hachette UK Company

www.hachette.co.uk
www.hachettechildrens.co.uk

The authorised representative in the EEA is
Hachette Ireland, 8 Castlecourt Centre,
Dublin 15, D15 XTP3, Ireland
(email: info@hbgi.ie)

GREAT SCIENTISTS

WANGARI MAATHAI

RUTH PERCIVAL AND ALEXANDRA BADIU

WAYLAND

On the 1st of April, 1940, Wangari Muta was born in a Kenyan village called Ihithe. This beautiful place sits among the lush forests and grasslands of Kenya's Central Highlands.

Wangari's family were farmers and members of Kenya's largest tribe – the Kikuyu. Kenya, in Africa, was ruled by the British Empire at this time. This meant that much of the best farming land was taken from Kenyans and given to white people from Britain.

Wangari in her garden

At the age of about 7, Wangari's mother gave her a small vegetable garden. Wangari loved to plant and care for her crops. But the landscape was changing. White settlers cut down thousands of native trees. In their place they planted fast-growing non-native trees to sell the wood. Young Wangari saw habitats destroyed and that this affected local people and wildlife.

Fig trees are important to Kikuyu culture, and one grew near Wangari's home. She knew never to chop wood from this tree, but she didn't know that a fig tree's deep roots can help to control the flow of water underground. Fig trees are one of the reasons that Wangari's homeland was so lush.

At this time, girls in Kenya were mostly taught to cook, sew and look after the home. Many didn't go to school, read or write, but Wangari's family wanted her to have an education. At the age of 8, Wangari went to Ihithe Primary School, where she learned English, Swahili and maths. When she turned 11, Wangari studied at a boarding school in the nearby town of Nyeri. Aged 16, she finished her exams and came top of her class.

Wangari then went to Loreto High School in Limuru, not far from Kenya's capital city, Nairobi. Here she continued to study hard.

A WONDERFUL HIGH SCHOOL SCIENCE TEACHER HELPED WANGARI TO DISCOVER HER TALENT FOR SCIENCE.

The 1950s, brought change to Africa. The British Empire and some European countries were losing control. Many African countries were winning back their independence. Change brought new opportunities for bright students like Wangari, too. An important Kenyan politician called Tom Mboya was trying to help young East Africans get into colleges and universities in the USA and Canada.

Tom Mboya

Dr Martin Luther King, Jr

President John F. Kennedy

Mboya set up a programme with help from some famous Black Americans, including the civil rights leader, Dr Martin Luther King, Jr. The US president, John F. Kennedy, helped to pay for the flights, which became known as the 'Kennedy Airlift'.

Wangari had won a scholarship to Mount St Scholastica College, in Kansas, USA. Here she studied biology, chemistry and German. Wangari graduated in 1964, a year after Kenya finally won back its independence from Britain in 1963.

In 1965, after graduating, Wangari moved to study at the University of Pittsburgh, in Pennsylvania, USA. Here she did a Masters in Biology and became a more skilled scientist. Pittsburgh at that time had many factories that polluted the air. It made the city dirty and the air dangerous to breathe.

WANGARI JOINED ACTIVISTS CAMPAIGNING FOR CLEANER AIR IN THE CITY.

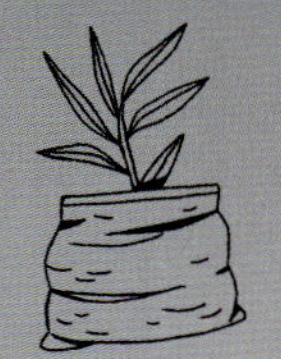

This was Wangari's first experience of a 'green' campaign. It would not be her last!

After Wangari graduated in January 1966, she returned to Kenya. She was supposed to start work as a research assistant for a zoology professor at University College, Nairobi. But when she got there, the job had been given to a man!

Wangari at the zoology department

By chance, Wangari met a German professor called Reinhold Hoffman. He was impressed by her scientific skills and qualifications, and that she spoke German. That year, Wangari became his assistant at the School of Animal Medicine at University College, Nairobi.

Soon, Wangari also began teaching biology there. She found it a challenge at first. Students and colleagues doubted her because she was a woman. They soon found out that Wangari was excellent at her job and she earned a lot of respect.

In April 1966, Wangari met Mwangi Mathai.
Three years later, in spring 1969, they married.

Wangari helped Mwangi to campaign for a seat
in parliament. It was a dangerous political time
in Kenya. Tom Mboya (see pages 8–9) was
assassinated. Mwangi failed to win a seat and
democracy ended in Kenya when President
Kenyatta decided that only his party was allowed
to exist.

In 1970, Wangari's son Waweru was born. All
this while, Wangari had also studied for a PhD in
veterinary anatomy. In 1971, she became the first
woman in East and Central Africa to receive a
PhD. In December that year, her first daughter,
Wanjira, was born.

Wangari receives
her PhD

Wangari spent a lot of time in the countryside for her work, studying diseases in cows. She noticed that the land she remembered as a child had changed. So many native trees had been chopped down that rainwater ran off the land, washing the soil away instead of soaking into the earth. The non-native trees that had been planted had shallow roots that couldn't hold the water back.

Everywhere, the forests and grasslands of her childhood were suffering. People were suffering too. The rivers were now muddy and many drinking water sources were polluted.

One day, Wangari went to visit her childhood fig tree.
But it had been cut down to make way for tea plants.
Many Kenyan farmers at this time grew tea and coffee
to be sold around the world. This brought in money, but
it meant that there was not enough land to grow food,
such as finger millet (a type of grain), for local people.

In 1972, Wangari joined the National Council of Women of Kenya (NCWK). At one meeting they talked about local children not getting enough food because the tea and coffee plantations took up so much land. Instead of growing most of their own food, people bought cheap bread and rice, which are less healthy foods than the traditionally grown grains and vegetables. Local people were suffering.

 WANGARI KNEW EXACTLY HOW TO SOLVE THE PROBLEM. THE ANSWER WAS TO PLANT NATIVE TREES! 

In 1975, Wangari set up Envirocare. The aim was simple: plant seedlings of native trees to help restore the forests. She was asked to talk about tree planting at a United Nations (UN) event in 1976. Even so, a lack of government support meant that Envirocare had to close.

Wangari didn't give up. On the 1st of January, 1977, she started the Green Belt Movement (GBM). On World Environment Day (5th of June) that year, hundreds of people marched to Kamukunji Park in Nairobi to plant seven trees – including an African fig tree – to honour each of Kenya's ethnic groups.

Tree-planting ceremony at Kamukunji Park

At first, people didn't understand why the GBM was so important. Yet by the end of 1977, word had spread. Farmers, schools and communities across Kenya slowly took up the cause.

Wangari wanted to plant a tree for every person
in Kenya – 15 million people – and asked the
government's forestry department for help.
At first, they gave her seedlings for free, but
later they wanted money for more seedlings.
So, Wangari took matters into her own hands.

WANGARI ASKED LOCAL WOMEN TO FIND
NATIVE TREE SEEDS IN LOCAL FORESTS
TO CREATE SEEDLING NURSERIES.

Lines of trees planted as a 'green belt'

In Kenya's climate, trees grow quickly. By planting more
than enough trees for fruit and wood, either to sell or use
themselves, these green belt forests were sustainable.

In July 1979, Wangari and Mwangi divorced. Wangari found the divorce court case difficult as it was held in public. At that time, women in Kenya were supposed to be quiet and not make a fuss, but it just made her more determined. After it was over, Wangari changed her surname from Mathai to Maathai.

In 1981 (until 1987), Wangari became the head of the NCWK. The GBM was becoming bigger and more successful. The Kenyan government didn't like that it was led by a woman.

Wangari left her university job to run for election to parliament the following year. Then, the government said that it was illegal for her to do this. The university wouldn't give her job back, so she turned all her attention to the GBM and wrote to the UN for support. Shortly after, the Norwegian Forestry Society got in touch, and offered her a job and to work with her.

By 1989, the GBM was working in other
African countries: Ethiopia, Tanzania,
Uganda, Rwanda and Mozambique.

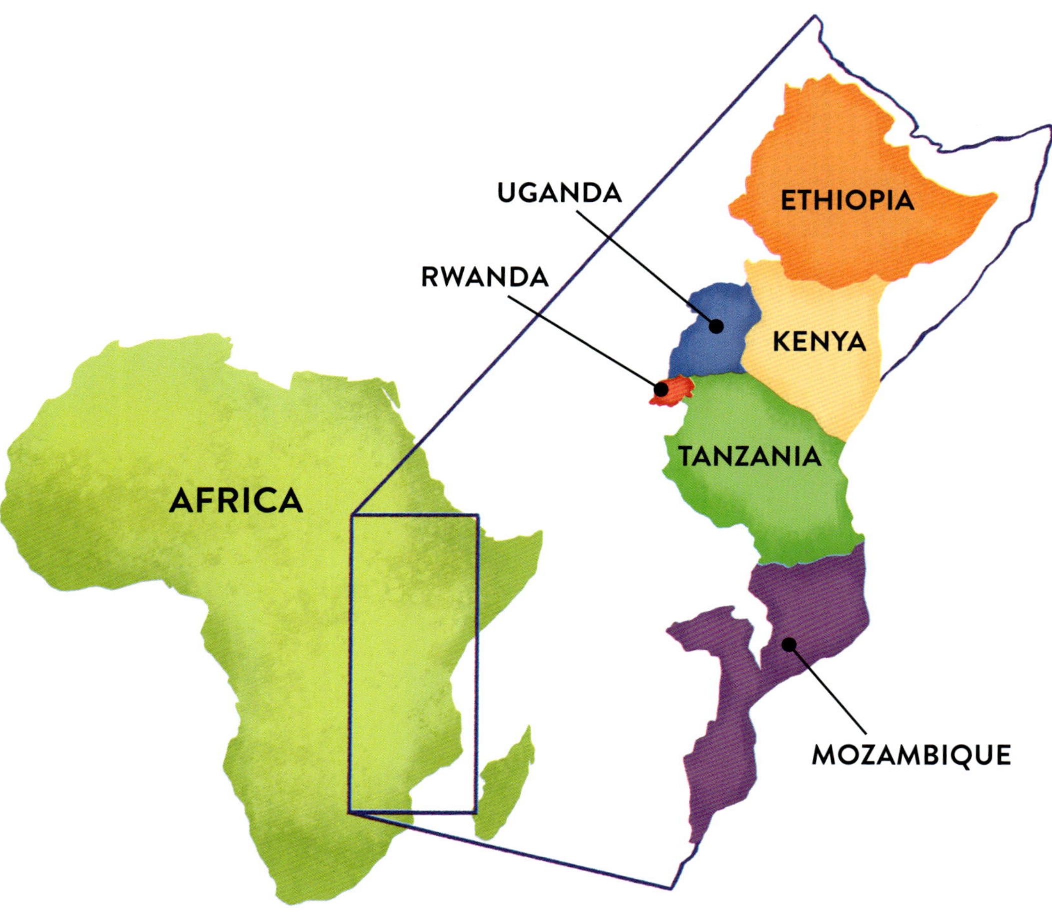

But there were still problems. Wangari did not like
that public lands, such as some parks and forests, were
sold to people who had friends in the government.
On this land, trees were chopped down to make way
for buildings and the Kenyan government still allowed
non-native trees to be planted in national forests.

Wangari continued to speak out. This was dangerous. Any criticism of the government could land her in prison. Yet she still chose to campaign against the building of a huge skyscraper in Uhuru Park in the middle of Nairobi. The government tried to stop Wangari from campaigning by having the police throw her out of her own office!

Wangari asked everyone she knew at the UN, and in countries such as Canada, the US and the UK, for help. They helped to put pressure on the Kenyan government to stop the building in the park.

Over the next 10 years, the fight for democracy in Kenya grew bigger. There were many protests, but little changed. Wangari protested too, and was arrested several times. Even so, she wasn't going to let politics stand in the GBM's way!

In 1998, the government gave away part of the Karura Forest, which lies just north of Nairobi. Private homes were to be built here. This forest is a source of water for four major Kenyan rivers and is home to rare native plants and animals.

Wangari went there herself to stop the building work. There, she was attacked and badly injured. However, with the pressure of the world watching, the Kenyan government backed down. Finally, in 1999, the president announced that no public land would be built on. It was another victory for Wangari and the GBM.

Wangari at a building site in Karura Forest

By this time, Wangari's much loved mother was very ill. Wangari cared for her until her death in March 2000.

In 2002, Wangari was elected to parliament, along with a new democratic president of Kenya. Times had finally changed. On the 8th of October, 2004, 74-year-old Wangari received wonderful news. She was to be awarded the Nobel Peace Prize! Wangari celebrated by planting a tree.

Wangari and her Nobel Peace Prize medal

Wangari never stopped working. She wrote several books, including *The Green Belt Movement* in 2004. Then in 2006, along with the UN, Wangari launched the Billion Tree Campaign. Sadly, Wangari died of cancer aged 71 on 25 September 2011. But she died knowing that far more than a billion trees had been planted worldwide. By December that year, the number stood at over 12 billion trees!

In 2020, a new campaign was launched to plant more than a trillion trees. This incredible aim traces its roots back to Wangari's love for her childhood fig tree and her passion for science and the environment.

TIMELINE

1940   Wangari Muta was born in Ihithe, Kenya, into the Kikuyu tribe.

1943   The family moved to a white-owned farm for Wangari's father to take up a new job.

1947   Wangari, her mother and two brothers moved back to Ihithe for the boys to go to primary school. Wangari was given a vegetable garden by her mother.

1948   Wangari started primary school.

1951–1956 Wangari went to boarding school in the town of Nyeri. After her exams, she finished top of her class.

1956–1960 Wangari attended high school in Limuru.

1960   Wangari was given a scholarship to study at university in Kansas, USA, and a place on Tom Mboya's 'Kennedy Airlift'.

1963   Kenya won back its independence from the UK.

1964   Wangari graduated with a science degree.

1965–1966 Wangari attended the University of Pittsburgh to study for a masters degree in biology. She campaigned for cleaner air in the city.

1966   Wangari graduated and returned to Kenya with a research job offer at University College, Nairobi. Wangari was told that the letter of the job offer wasn't official because it was handwritten. Wangari stayed with a relative in Nairobi and she met professor Reinhold Hoffman. He offered her a job as a research assistant at the School of Animal Medicine at University College, Nairobi. She taught and studied for her PhD. She met Mwangi Mathai the same year.

1967–1970 Wangari went to Germany to study for her PhD. In spring 1969, she returned and married Mwangi to become Wangari Mathai. In July 1969, Tom Mboya was assassinated. Wangari's son, Waweru was born in December 1970.

1971   Wangari was the first woman in East and Central Africa to receive a PhD (Veterinary Anatomy). Her first daughter, Wanjira was born.

1971   Wangari noticed changes in the landscape while at work.

1972   Wangari joined the NCWK. Discussions about local problems helped her to realise that planting native trees would help.

1974   Wangari's third child, Muta was born.

1975   Wangari started Envirocare to create nurseries of native tree seedlings and plant them to restore forests.

1976   In June that year, Wangari attended the UN conference on settlements – called Habitat I.

1977–1979 Wangari started the Green Belt Movement (GBM). She became the Associate Professor of the Department of Veterinary Anatomy. The GBM spread. The government gave her free seedlings at first, but later wanted payment for them. Wangari got local women to collect native seeds to grow seedlings instead. Wangari and Mwangi divorced in 1979. She added an 'a' to her name: Maathai.

1981   Wangari was chair of the NCWK (until 1987). The government withdrew money and support for the GBM.

1981   Wangari left her university job to run for election. The government said this was illegal. The Norwegian Forestry Society asked to work with her and the GBM grew.

1981–1989 The GBM expanded to other East African nations. In Kenya, Wangari campaigned for building work to stop in national forests and on public lands. In response, the government threw her out of her offices.

1989–1998 Wangari continued to campaign and plant trees even though it was dangerous to do so. She was arrested several times. Wangari got more involved in politics and ran for election to parliament in 1987. She lost.

1999   Wangari went to Karura Forest and demanded that building work there stopped. Finally, the government backed down.

2000   Wangari's mother died.

2002   Wangari was elected to parliament.

2004   Wangari received the Nobel Peace Prize.

2006   Wangari launched the Billion Tree Campaign with the UN.

2011   Wangari died. Twelve billion trees had been planted by this time.

QUIZ

1. Where was Wangari born?

2. What did Wangari's mother give her when she was 7 years old?

3. What type of tree is important to Kikuyu culture?

4. Why were native trees being cut down in Kenya?

5. What was Wangari's first experience of a 'green' campaign?

6. What does GBM stand for?

7. How many major rivers flow through the Karura Forest?

8. What did Wangari stop from being built in the Karura Forest?

9. How did Wangari celebrate her Nobel Prize?

10. When Wangari died in 2011, how many trees had been planted by the Billion Tree Campaign?

The answers are on page 32.

GLOSSARY

activist a person who campaigns for change.

assassinated when a person is killed by a rival for that rival's benefit, often for political reasons.

British Empire the countries and lands around the world ruled by the UK between 1583 and 1987.

civil rights the rights to freedom and equality.

democracy a system of government where members are fairly elected by the people; social equality.

ethnic a group of people who share culture and ancestors.

illegal against the law.

independence for a country, this means ruling itself instead of being ruled by another country.

native a person or other living thing that is born or naturally grows or lives in an area.

PhD the highest degree that can awarded by a university.

plantation a place (often run by one family) where a single crop, such as sugar or tea, is grown and workers pick the crop.

scholarship money to pay for a student's education, usually for bright students who cannot afford to pay themselves.

settler a person who moves from one country to live in another.

sustainable something that is able to stay the same without harming itself or the environment.

Swahili an East-African language used by millions of people. It is also called Kiswahili.

tribe a group of people within a country or area, usually made up of families and communities who share a culture and language.

veterinary anatomy the study of animal bodies.

zoology the scientific study of animals.

INDEX

Answers to quiz (page 30):
1. Ihithe village, Kenya; 2. a vegetable garden; 3. fig tree, ; 4. to make room for fast-growing non-native trees to be planted; 5. a clean air campaign in Pittsburgh, USA; 6. Green Belt Movement; 7. four; 8. private homes; 9. she planted a tree; 10. 12 billion trees.